OXFORI

SECOND
LITTLE BOOK
OF
POETRY

Chosen by John Foster

Contents

OXFORD
UNIVERSITY PRESS

The Crocodile is Coming

The crocodile is coming!
It's heading for the pool,
It's swaying down the road
From the local Primary School.
Better keep your distance,
Better close your doors –
Beware the fearful clamour
From its ever-open jaws!
Be careful not to stumble
As you hurry from the street:
Remember that the crocodile
Has sixty tramping feet!
Through the city jungle
The creature marches on.
Wisely, shoppers stand aside
And wait until it's gone.

It's going to cross the busy street –
It starts to leave the path –
Attacked by snarling traffic
It's completely cut in half –
The head continues on its way,
The tail, delayed, just laughs
And runs to catch it up
At the Municipal Baths.
The crocodile is swimming
In the Public Swimming Pool,
But soon it will be heading
For the local Primary School.
So, better keep your distance,
Better if you try
To find a place to hide
While the crocodile goes by!

June Crebbin

Roger the Dog

Asleep he wheezes at his ease.
He only wakes to scratch his fleas.

He hogs the fire, he bakes his head
As if it were a loaf of bread.

He's just a sack of snoring dog.
You can lug him like a log.

You can roll him with your foot,
He'll stay snoring where he's put.

I take him out for exercise,
He rolls in cowclap up to his eyes.

He will not race, he will not romp,
He saves his strength for gobble and chomp.

He'll work as hard as you could wish
Emptying his dinner dish,

Then flops flat, and digs down deep,
Like a miner, into sleep.

Ted Hughes

The Corn Scratch Kwa Kwa Hen and the Fox

And the Corn Scratch Kwa Kwa Hen
Heard the grumbling rumbling belly
Of the Slink Back Brush Tail Fox
A whole field away.

And she said to her sisters in the henhouse,
"Sisters, that Slink Back Brush Tail Fox
Will come and here's what we must do,"
And she whispered in their sharp sharp ears, "kwa, kwa".

And when that Slink Back Brush Tail Fox
Came over the field at night,
She heard his paw slide on a leaf,
And the Corn Scratch Kwa Kwa Hen and her sisters
Opened their beaks and —

"KWA!"
The moon jumped
And the Chooky Chook Chicks
Hid under the straw and giggled,
It was the LOUDEST KWA in the world.

And the Log Dog and the Scat Cat
And the Brat Rat and the House Mouse
And the Don't Harm Her Farmer
And his Life Wife and their Shorter Daughter
And their One Son came running,

On their slip slop, flip flop,
Scatter clatter, slick flick, tickly feet
And they opened their mouths and shouted –

"FOX!"
And it was the LOUDEST NAME in the world.
Then the Slink Back Brush Tail Fox
Ran over the fields and far away
And hid in a hole with his grumbling rumbling belly.

And the Corn Scratch Kwa Kwa Hen
Tucked the Chooky Chook Chicks under her feathers
And said "kwa",
And it was the softest kwa in the world.

Julie Holder

I am the Rain

I am the rain
I like to play games
like sometimes I pretend
I'm going to
                fall
Man that's the time
I don't come at all

Like sometimes
I get these laughing stitches
up my sides
rushing people in
                and out
with the clothesline

I just love
                drip
                dropping
                down
                collars
                and spines

Maybe it's a shame
but it's the only way
I get some fame

Grace Nichols

The Rainbow

The rainbow's like a coloured bridge
that sometimes shines from ridge to ridge.
Today one end is in the sea,
the other's in this field with me.

Iain Crichton-Smith

Magic Horse

Black horse,
Magic horse,
Carry me away,
Over the river,
Across the bay
To the sandy beach
Where I can play.

Black horse,
Magic horse,
Carry me away,
Over the seas
To the forest trees
Where I can watch
The tiger cubs play.

Black horse,
Magic horse,
Carry me away
To Arctic snows
Where the cold wind blows
Where I can watch
The polar bears play.

Black horse,
Magic horse
Carry me away
To golden sands
In far-away lands
Where the sea is blue
And I can play all day.

John Foster

The Snowman

He shines like a candle
and melts slowly

He is white and black
and gets smaller all the time

He is as white as feathers
and white horses and snow

He glows in the dark
like a glow-worm

He stands on a flat place
and makes a shadow in the light

He crumples in a circle
like a circus tent

He turns to ice and slush
like a camel's hump

He runs away like milk
and melts like moonlight in sunshine

In the morning he is gone
like the moon.

Gillian Clarke

What is Red?

Red is a sunset
Blazing and bright.
Red is feeling brave
With all your might.
Red is a sunburn
Spot on your nose.
Sometimes red
Is a red red rose.
Red squiggles out
When you cut your hand.
Red is a brick
And the sound of a band.
Red is hotness
You get inside
When you're embarrassed
And want to hide.
Fire-cracker, fire-engine
Fire-flicker red—

And when you're angry
Red runs through your head.
Red is an Indian,
A Valentine heart,
The trimmings on
A circus cart.
Red is a lipstick
Red is a shout
Red is a signal
That says: "Watch out!"
Red is a great big
Rubber ball.
Red is the giant-est
Colour of all.
Red is a show-off,
No doubt about it—
But can you imagine
Living without it?

Mary O'Neill

Happy Birthday Card

H appy birthday, all of us say
A nd may you have a lovely day.
P lenty of nice dreams!
P resents and ice creams!
Y ucky buns!
B est of fun!
I nteresting invitations!
R ailway stations!
T elly and trips!
H amburgers and chips! BUT
D o get a cough (if) –
A nd I hope your knees fall off (if)
Y ou forget mine

Rony Robinson

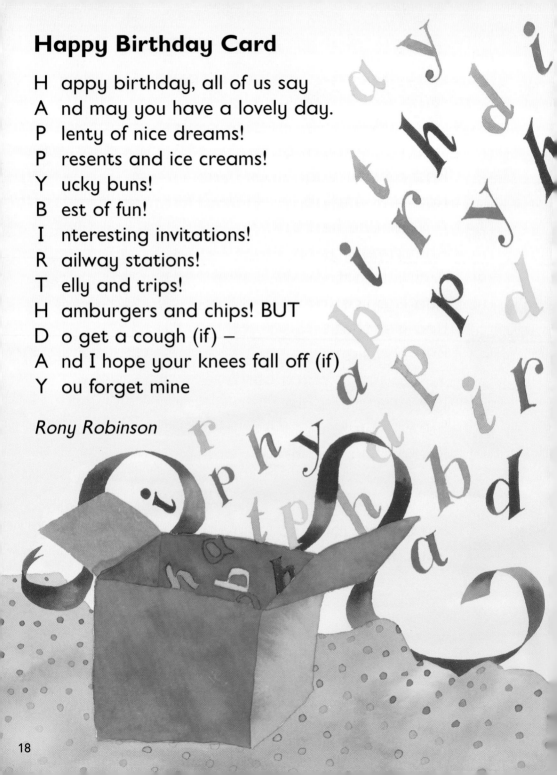

Ways of the Week

Sunday
Good-to-be-done day.

Monday
Skipping and fun day.

Tuesday
Fall, blackened bruise day.

Wednesday
Clucking old hen's day.

Thursday
Purring, warm fur's day.

Friday
Can't-make-me-cry day.

Saturday
Just doesn't matter day.

John Kitching

Calendar of Clothes

January is a time for coats,
for caps and fur-lined boots.

February likes hats with flaps
and zipped up coloured ski suits.

March can do with anoraks
and jeans and woolly tops.

April needs a change of clothes
for sun and wind and raindrops.

May brings cotton tee-shirts
with jumpers still on hand.

By June the skirts are skimpy,
shorts short for playing on sand.

July comes along in bathing trunks,
and caps with dark green shades.

August gets the sunsuits out
with balls and buckets and spades.

September, and it's back to school,
uniform, shirt and stripey tie.

October brings scarves out again
as leaves whirl up to the sky.

November means turned-up collars
against wind and fog and storm.

December shakes out party frocks.
Christmas fun keeps everyone warm.

Moira Andrew

Giant Tale

He was …

As wide as an oak tree,
tall as a willow;
his snore was the thunder,
a mountain his pillow.

Each step brought an earthquake,
each breath blew a gale;
one laugh moved an ocean,
each tear filled a pail.

His mouth was a crater,
with snakes for a tongue;
his eyes were the size
of the earth and the sun.

One toe was as heavy
as Venus and Mars;
his forehead was Saturn,
his hair shone with stars.

Judith Nicholls

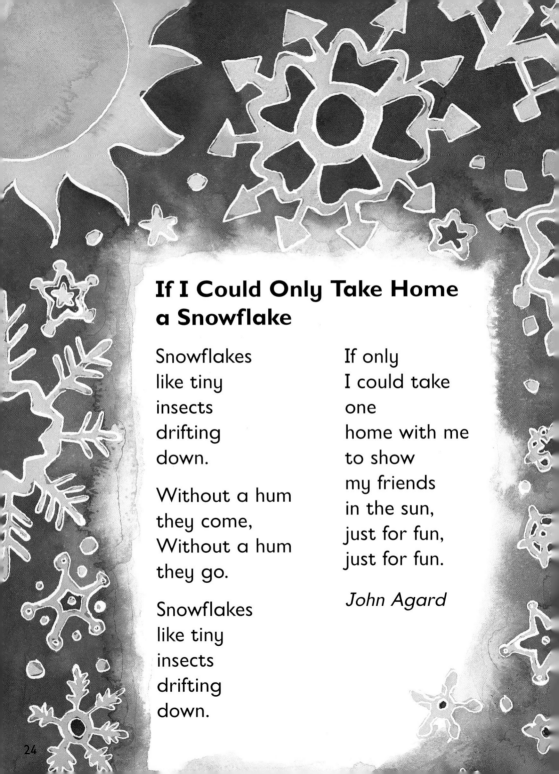

If I Could Only Take Home a Snowflake

Snowflakes
like tiny
insects
drifting
down.

Without a hum
they come,
Without a hum
they go.

Snowflakes
like tiny
insects
drifting
down.

If only
I could take
one
home with me
to show
my friends
in the sun,
just for fun,
just for fun.

John Agard